THE LAW OF GOD

FOR CHILDREN

by Galina Kalinina

illustrated by Victor Domin

Grand Rapids · Exaltation Press · 2019

As retold by: Galina Kalinina
Illustrator: Victor Domin
Translator: Fr. John Hogg

"The Law of God for Children"
    This book is designed to introduce children to the foundations of the Orthodox faith in a simple and accessible format and to help them understand the most important truths of the Gospel: love for God and our neighbor, mercy, compassion, and hope. Children who grow up in this modern world often have serious and pressing questions that adults sometimes find difficult to answer. Our book will try to help.

Translated from the original "Закон Божий для Детей" by Lepta Press, Copyright © Trading house «Лепта», http://www.lepta-kniga.ru/

ISBN: 978-1-950067-82-4 (Paperback)

Edited by Anna Lichtenstein

First printing edition 2019

Exaltation Press
Grand Rapids, MI

www.ExaltationPress.com

For bulk orders, please contact editor@exaltationpress.com.

Table of Contents

Chapter One

How Do We Know About God?

The Maker and Creator of our world has given us, human beings, the ability to learn about Him. To do that, He has given us two marvelous "books." One "book" is nature – the world around us, which reflects His power and wisdom like in a mirror. The other book is the Bible, written by wise people with His guidance. This book reveals His will. What does the "book of nature" tell us? You've probably often asked those older than you where the world came from. How did the stars, the clouds, the flowers and trees, the birds and animals, and we ourselves, human beings, appear?

Some people think that everything in the universe was formed by itself. But is that believable? For example, is it really believable to think that a beautiful painting painted itself? Or to look at a palace and think that it built itself? Just like a painting is made by an artist, a book by an author, a house by an architect and construction workers, and a car by engineers and skilled workers, the same thing is true about nature. The universe has to have a Maker, a Creator. In English, we call Him

"God." Each language has its own word for this Creator.

"But has anyone ever seen Him?," you might ask.

"No, it's impossible to see Him with our eyes. He is invisible."

"But things that are invisible only exist in fairy tales!"

"Not only in fairy tales. The invisible exists. And what is invisible is what is most amazing and most important in our life."

Imagine for a moment that you're thinking about last summer and dreaming that next year, you'll also be able to go swimming in the sea or hiking in the woods. You may have happy thoughts or sad thoughts. But none of them can be seen. You can only see the expression on your face or hear the words that you say when you have those thoughts. But your mind, your thoughts, and your feelings are what make you a human being. That means that the invisible does exist. Without it, we wouldn't be people.

The creator of the world is unseen, just like your thoughts, but we do see before our eyes His numberless creations. And we should give Him thanks for everything: for the bright morning, for the rain and sunshine, for the joy of being alive. How great and vast God's world is! The world can't be counted or measured and only the God who made it knows the measure, weight, and quantity of it all. God created this whole world for us to live in and use. He created it for each of us. That is how limitless God's love for us is! And if we love God and live according to His laws, then many things in the world that we don't understand will become clear and understandable to us. If we love God and live with everyone else in friendship, love, and joy, then that joy will never end and nobody will be able to take it away from us, because God Himself will be with us.

Mankind is able to talk to God. Our conversation with Him is called "prayer." When we trust our Creator, when we desire to live according to His will, and when we love Him, that is called "faith."

Prayer, at home and at Church, keeping God's commandments, the feasts, services, and traditions that remind us about God – all of that together is called "religion." God Himself reveals many things to mankind through those that He sends, saints and wise men. The Bible contains the most important things that He reveals to us.

The Bible teaches us how to do what is right and how to tell right from wrong. It teaches us how we should treat each other, living things, and the whole creation around us. People learned all of this gradually. God spent a long time teaching mankind so that we would understand and master this most important science. And truthfully, it wasn't easy.

For God has revealed that He doesn't want to make us live according to His law by force. He wants us to receive His teaching voluntarily. He created our soul according to His likeness and that means that He gave us the gift of freedom. We often misuse our freedom. We become capricious and headstrong. We turn away from God and don't want to follow His word. And of course, when we do that, we simply harm ourselves. But the Creator waits patiently, from time to time showing us where malice, lies, greed, cowardice, harshness, and laziness can lead us. The Bible tells us about all of this. The word "Bible" is a Greek word that in English means "Book." The Bible is a book that is made up of many books, written by outstanding people. They wrote for many years, over a thousand years.

The chief part of the Bible is called the Gospel. In Greek, that is "Evangelion," a word that means "Good News." "Gospel" also means "good news," but it comes from Old English. What good news? The news that the Creator loves the whole world and each person. That He can free us from evil. That once, He Himself appeared among men to speak to them face-to-face. In a word, it is the news about Christ. The Gospel was composed by those who knew Him personally, His disciples. But in order for us to remember that we belong to God, to be closer to Him and to love Him (or, in other words, in order for us to fulfill our destiny here on earth and then go to meet God in the Kingdom of Heaven) we need to know more about God. We need to know His will – we need to know the Law of God.

Chapter Two

God

God created the whole world out of nothing, by His word alone. He can do anything that He desires.

God is the highest Being. He has no equal, neither on earth nor in heaven. We human beings cannot fully understand Him with our mind. And we couldn't learn anything about Him by ourselves if God Himself had not revealed Himself to us. Everything that we know about Him, He has revealed to us.

When God created the first people, Adam and Eve, He appeared to them in Paradise and taught them about Himself, how He created the world, how they should have faith in the One True God and how to do His will. At first, this divine teaching was passed on orally, from generation to generation and then later, by God's inspiration, it was written down in sacred books. Finally, the Son of God Himself, Jesus Christ, appeared on earth and gave us the rest of the knowledge that we need about God. After He ascended into heaven, the Holy Spirit revealed even more divine wisdom to the Apostles, who wrote it down in the "Epistles" which are the last part of the Bible.

He revealed to mankind the great mystery that God is one in three Persons. The First Person is God the Father, the second Person is God the Son, and the third Person is God the Holy Spirit. They aren't three gods but one God in three Persons, the Trinity one in essence and undivided. All three Persons have the same divine dignity, and none of them is older or younger than the others. Just like God the Father is the true God, so also God the Son is the true God and God the Holy Spirit is the true God.

> The word "essence" means being. A useful way to think about it is that in God, there is only one "what" but there are three "whos."

By revealing to us the mystery of the Most-Holy Trinity, Jesus Christ taught us not only to worship God in truth but also to love Him, since all three Persons of the Most-Holy Trinity – the Father, the Son, and the Holy Spirit – exist eternally in unceasing love towards each other and together make up one Being. God is perfect love.

St. Cyril, the enlightener of the Slavs, tried to explain the mystery of the Most-Holy Trinity like this: "Do you see in the shining disk in the sky, the sun, and the light and heat that proceed from it? God the Father is like that shining disk, but without beginning or end. His Son is eternally begotten from Him, just like the light that is always coming from the sun. And just like not only light but also heat comes from the sun, so also the Holy Spirit proceeds from the Father. Each of us can distinguish the disk of the sun, its light and its heat, but they aren't three suns. There is only one sun in the sky. It's the same with the Holy Trinity. There are three Persons but God is one and undivided."

> *In Orthodox theology, the word "mystery" does not mean something mysterious but something mystical, something that cannot be understood by reason alone but that has to be revealed by God Himself. It also refers to what are often called the Sacraments, like Baptism and the Eucharist, the special means by which God mystically infuses us with His Grace.*

This great mystery that God has revealed

to us about Himself, the mystery of the Holy Trinity, is one that our weak, human minds cannot contain or explain with words. But we can learn it and perceive it with our heart and soul through experience.

Chapter Three

The Characteristics of God

God – the Most-Holy Trinity – has revealed to us about Himself that He is "bodiless and unseen (cf. John 4:24)." That means that God doesn't have a body, skin, or bones like we have. God is not made out of anything that our visible world is

> Although according to His divinity, God is Spirit and has no body, when Christ, the Son of God, becomes Man, He does have a human body.

made up of, and for that reason, we cannot see Him with our eyes.

To explain this, let's look at an example from our earthly world. Although we can't see the air, we do see its actions and effects. The movement of the air (the wind) is very strongand able to move, for example, a large ship. We feel the air and know that we breathe air and can't live without it. In the same way, although we don't see God, we see His actions and manifestations. His wisdom and power are everywhere in the world, and we can perceive them in ourselves as well.

But the unseen God, out of His love for us, has sometimes appeared to certain righteous people in a visible way, like in a reflection, making it so they could see Him by His mercy. Otherwise, they would have perished from His greatness and glory. God said to Moses, "You cannot see my face, for man shall not see me and live" (Ex. 33:20). If the sun can blind us with its brilliance so that we cannot look directly at it, although it is a created thing, how much more are we unable to look at God, who created the sun!

God is eternal
(Ps. 89:3; Ex. 40:28)

"Eternal" means that God always exists.

Everything that we see in the world began to exist at some point, was born, and will someday end, die, or be destroyed. In this world, everything is temporary. Everything has a beginning and an end. At one time, there was neither heaven nor earth, nor even time. There was only God alone because He is without beginning: no one created Him. And since He has no beginning, He is without end as well. God has always been and always will be. That is why we call Him "eternal."

God is unchanging
(James 1:17, Mal. 3:6)

"Unchanging" means that God is always the same.

In this world, everything is always changing: nature, animals, people... Water flows, clouds sometimes appear in the sky, sometimes gather into big rain clouds, and sometimes disappear completely. Plants and animals are born, grow, become old, and then die. The same thing is true about people, about you and me. In the world, one thing is always replaced by another.

Only God is constant. In Him there is no changing. He doesn't grow, He doesn't get old, and He will never change at all. He is now the way that He always was and will remain the same forever. That is why we call Him "unchanging."

God is all-powerful
(Gen. 17:1; Luke 1:37)

"All-powerful" means that God can do whatever He desires. Nothing is impossible for Him.

If we want to do something, we need the material, the time, the power, and the knowledge. If we're missing something, if we don't have enough material or if we haven't learned how to do something, then what we want to do won't be possible, or will not be as good as we want it to be. We can do many things. For example, with the help of paint, we can paint beautiful pictures on canvas, or we can take metal and make complicated and useful machines. But we can never, for example, create the earth that we live on, the sun that shines on us and warms us, or many other things.

Only God has nothing that He is unable to do. He wanted to create the world and then it was created from nothing by His word alone. That is why we call Him "all-powerful."

God is everywhere present
(Ps. 138:7-12)

God always, at all times, is present everywhere. There is nowhere in the whole world that He is not. No person or place can hide from Him.

God is everywhere. That is why we call Him "everywhere present."

God is omniscient
(1 John 3:20; Heb. 4:13)

"Omniscient" means that God always hears, sees, and knows everything. A person can learn many things, find out a lot of information, but no person can ever know everything. In addition, we can't know the future or see and hear everything that is happening in every corner of the world.

Only God knows everything. He knows what was, what is, and what will be. For God, there is no difference between day and night. At all times, He sees and hears all things. He knows each of us. He doesn't only know what we do and say but also what we think and what we desire. He knows what has happened to us in the past and He knows what the future holds for us. That is why we call Him "omniscient" – "all-knowing".

God is all-good
(Matt. 19:17)

The word "all-good" means that He is the best and the kindest.

People aren't always kind. It often happens that we don't like a particular person. Only God loves us all to the highest degree, in a way that no human being can love. He gives us everything that we need for life. Everything that we see in Heaven and on earth, the Lord created for the good, the use, and the joy of human beings.

The first things that God gave us are life and a rational (thinking) soul that is able to reason and learn, as well as a heart that is capable of loving.

God gave us everything to support and sustain our life. His gifts include the air, light, and water that we couldn't live without. It includes every kind of food that we

It is human sin and greed, hoarding what God gives to all people, that create any kind of scarcity.

need to preserve our life. We have a mom and a dad, friends, and many of us have brothers and sisters. How much joy, help, and comfort these people bring us! But we wouldn't have any of them if God hadn't given them to us.

God is always ready to give us every good thing. He cares about us more than the best father cares about his children. That is why we call God "all-good" or "most-merciful." And that is why we call Him our Heavenly Father.

God is all-righteous
(Ps. 7:12; Ps. 10:7)

People often don't tell the truth or are unjust. God, however, is just (fair) to the highest degree. He always judges people with righteousness. He doesn't punish people who behave well and do good works without reason, but He also doesn't leave any bad deed unpunished if we don't correct our lives through repentance and good works.

That is why we call God "all-righteous."

God is sufficient in Himself
(Acts 17:25)

As human beings, we are always in need of something, and so our desires are often unsatisfied.

Only God has all things, is satisfied, and doesn't need anything for Himself. On the contrary, He gives all things to all people. That is why we say that He is "sufficient in Himself."

God is most-blessed

God is not only sufficient in Himself but also always has in Himself the highest joy, the highest degree of happiness. That is why we call Him "most blessed."

But we human beings can never find true joy anywhere in life except in God.

We call God the Maker or Creator because He created the whole world, visible and invisible.

We also call Him the Almighty, our Master and King, because by His all-powerful will, He reigns and rules over everything that He created.

Chapter Four

Angels and Demons

In the beginning, when neither the world nor mankind existed, God created the holy angels. Angels are spirits that are bodiless (which is why they are invisible) and immortal, like our souls. They have been given the gift of mind, will, and power. God created them as a numberless host. They always do the will of God. They are sinless, and now the grace of God has so strengthened them in doing good that they are not able to sin.

All the angels were created good and created to love God and each other, and from that life lived in love, they experienced ceaseless great joy. But God did not want to make them love Him by force, and so He gave them the ability to choose freely whether or not they themselves wanted to love Him.

One of them, named Lucifer, the highest and most powerful angel, was puffed up with pride at his power and strength, and so he refused to love God and do His will because he wanted to become like God. He began to slander God, to oppose everything God wanted, and to contradict Him. And so he became a dark, evil spirit – the Devil, Satan. The word "devil" means "slanderer" and the word "Satan" means "adversary." He is the adversary of God and of all that is good. This evil spirit seduced many other angels and led them astray with him. For opposing God, all of these angels lost the light and blessedness (i.e. joy) that they had been given and became evil, dark spirits, too. They are now called devils or demons.

One of God's chief angels, the Archangel Michael, stood against Satan and said, "Who is like God? No one is like God!" And a war took place in Heaven. Michael and his angels fought against Satan and his demons. The power of evil couldn't stand against the angels of God, and Satan fell with all of his demons to the underworld, to Hell. "Hell" or "the underworld" is a place far from God, which is where the evil spirits now abide. There, they are tormented by their own malice, seeing their powerlessness against God. They have become hardened in evil, so that now they cannot be good. They use deceit and cunning to try to lead each of us astray, instill in us evil thoughts and desires, so that we might perish.

And that rebellion of Lucifer's is how evil entered God's creation. "Evil" means everything that is done against God, everything that doesn't follow His will.

But all the angels who remained faithful to God have lived with God ever since in unceasing love and joy. The English word "angel" is derived from a Greek word meaning "messenger." That is because God sometimes sends angels to announce His will to people. In those cases, angels might take a visible, usually human-like form.

At our baptism, God gives each of us a guardian angel who invisibly protects us during our whole earthly life from misfortune and assaults of the enemy, who corrects us when we sin, and who guards us at the fearful hour of our death and who doesn't abandon us after death either.

In icons, angels are depicted as beautiful youths, which symbolizes their spiritual beauty. Their wings mean that they are quick to do the will of God.

Chapter Five

The Image of God in Man: The Soul

We know from the Bible that the Lord created human beings according to His image and likeness. The image of God in us is that which makes us resemble God. It includes our free will, since we ourselves decide what to do and what not to do; our minds, since no other living thing on earth has a mind like human beings do; and our ability to make things, to create and invent things that never before existed. Even our capacity for laughter and joy is from God.

But the most important part of our likeness to God is our ability to commune with Him and love the truth. Where is the image of God "located"? It is found in the human soul. The human soul is an immortal, intelligent power that governs the body. Our "me," our "self," is also contained in the soul – our unique personhood. In the whole world, none of us is the exactly same as anyone else. It is because of our souls that we are self aware. That self-awareness comes through using one of the soul's powers – reason.

The human soul isn't created out of matter,

the way everything in the physical world is, and so it can't be found by any instruments or tests. The human soul belongs to the spiritual world, the world of God and the angels. The human body, just like the bodies of all living things, is made out of matter, and when the soul leaves the body after death, the body decays into its constitutive elements, all the things like chemicals that earthly matter is made of.

And so, mankind lives in two worlds at the same time: the physical world and the spiritual world. Thanks to that duality, we can rejoice in the world that surrounds us, but we should never forget that our true home is in the spiritual world.

Chapter Six

Sin and the Fall of the First Human Beings

Sin, or evil, is the breaking of God's law and the violation of His will. Who was the first to break God's will? Satan, the Devil. But he taught people as well not to obey God. He taught them to sin and led them astray. Through craftiness and deceit, he taught Adam and Eve, the first people that God had created, to disobey God's will.

Sin is our rejection of life according to God's will, so it is already its own punishment. When we sin, we harm ourselves. Remember, mankind was created by God and established according to fixed laws. If we compare man to some sort of object, we will see that both man and, for example, a computer are both designed and work according to fixed rules. And if we break the rules of how a computer is supposed to work and suddenly start pouring water on it or dropping it on the floor then, of course, it will break. The same thing happened to humanity. Adam and Eve believed the devil and broke God's prohibition, and when they did, they didn't harm God, but themselves. Having broken themselves, they were no longer able to "fix" themselves and become like they once were.

But in His mercy, God has helped mankind by sending His Son, our Savior, Jesus Christ, to earth.

The Devil envied the bliss that the first people had in Paradise, and decided to take that life of Paradise away from them. To do that, he entered into a serpent and hid himself in the branches of the Tree of the Knowledge of Good and Evil. And when Eve was walking nearby, he began to try to convince her to eat the fruit of the tree. God had told Adam and Eve not to eat fruit from this tree. Satan cunningly asked Eve, "Is it true that God has forbidden you to eat from any of the trees in Paradise?"

"No," Eve answered the serpent, "We can eat the fruit of any of the trees. God said, 'Only of the fruit of the tree in the middle of Paradise shall you not eat nor touch lest you die.'"

But the Devil began to lie to lead Eve astray. He said, "No, you won't die. God knows that if you taste it, then you will become like gods and will know good and evil."

His cunning speech worked on Eve. She looked at the tree and saw that it was pleasant to look at, good to eat, and that it gave knowledge. She wanted to know good and evil. Eve picked some fruit from the forbidden tree and ate it and then gave some to her husband, Adam, who also ate.

And so, humanity gave in to the Devil's temptation and broke God's commandment, His will, and they fell into sin. That is how we fell.

This first sin, the sin of Adam and Eve, the Fall, is also called the "primordial sin," because it was that sin that was the beginning of all the other sins of mankind.

Some non-orthodox Christians also call it the "original sin." "Primordial" and "original" (as used here) are both words for "at the beginning of time" or "very ancient."

Chapter Seven

The Consequences of the Fall and the Promise of a Savior

When the first people sinned, they were ashamed and afraid, just like what always happens when someone behaves badly. They immediately noticed that they were naked. In order to hide their nakedness, they sewed clothing for themselves out of fig leaves, in the form of wide belts. Instead of them receiving the divine perfection like they had wanted, everything turned out in reverse. Their reason was darkened, their consciences began to torment them, and they lost their peace of soul.

All of this took place because they learned good and evil by means of a sin, against the will of God.

Sin changed them so much that when they heard the voice of God in Paradise, they hid themselves among the trees in fear and shame. They had immediately forgotten that nothing and nowhere is hidden from God, who is everywhere present and Who sees all things. This is an example of how each sin takes us away from God.

But God, in His mercy, began to call them to repentance. He wanted them to understand their sin, take responsibility for it before the Lord, and ask for forgiveness.

From the third chapter of Genesis

The Lord said, "Adam, where are you?"

Adam answered, "I heard Your voice in the garden and was afraid because I'm naked, and so I hid myself."

God asked again, "Who told you that you were naked? Did you eat the fruit of the tree that I forbade you to eat?"

But Adam said, "The wife that You gave me, she gave me the fruit and I ate it." And so Adam began to put the blame on Eve and even on God who had given him a wife.

And the Lord said to Eve, "What is this that you have done?"

To "seduce" means to lead someone astray, to convince them to do something wrong.

But instead of repenting, Eve said, "The serpent seduced me and I ate."

Then the Lord told them the consequences of the sin that they had committed.

God said to Eve, "In pain you will give birth to children and you will have to obey your husband."

He said to Adam, "Because of your sin, the

earth will not be as fertile as before. It will bring forth thorns and thistles for you. In the sweat of your brow you will eat your bread," or in other words, they would have to work hard to get their food, "until you return to the earth from which you were taken," that is, until they died. "For dust you are and to dust you shall return."

And to the devil, hidden in the serpent, who was most to blame for the humanity's sin, God said, "Cursed are you for having done this," and He said that there would be a battle between Satan and mankind, and that man would be the winner: "The seed of the woman will bruise your head and you will bite his heel." In other words, the woman would have a Descendant, the Savior of the World, who would be born of a virgin and defeat the devil and save mankind but in order to do that, He Himself would have to suffer. Humanity received this promise from God about the coming of a Savior with faith and joy and it gave them great comfort. And so that they wouldn't forget His promise, God taught mankind to offer sacrifices. He commanded them to slaughter a bull, lamb, or goat and to burn it with a prayer for the forgiveness of sins and with faith in the future Savior. Those sacrifices were a sign and an image of the Savior who would suffer and shed His blood for our sins, cleansing our souls from sin by His precious blood, making them pure, holy, and once again worthy of Paradise.

The first sacrifice for the sins of mankind was made there in Paradise, and then God took the skins of those animals and made clothing for Adam and Eve and dressed them.

But since humanity had become sinful, they were no longer able to live in Paradise. Sin had changed their nature and they were no longer the same as they had been. And so the Lord expelled them from Paradise and put a Cherub, an angel, at the entrance into Paradise with a flaming sword, to guard the way to the tree of life. Adam and Eve's primordial sin, with all of its consequences, was passed on to all of their descendants by natural birth. In other words, it was passed to all of humanity, to each of us. That is why we are born sinful and subject to all the consequences of sins – afflictions, sicknesses, and death.

And so the consequences of the Fall into sin turned out to be great and terrible. Mankind was deprived of the blessed life of Paradise. The world, ruined by sin, was changed. From that time on, the land began to yield crops only with great effort. Instead of bringing forth good fruits, weeds began to grow in the fields. Animals began to fear human beings and became wild predators. Sickness, suffering, and death appeared. But most important of all, through their sinfulness, human beings lost the ability to communicate with God face to face, the way Adam and Eve spoke to Him in Paradise. God no longer appeared to people in a visible way; the sight of God became intolerable for our souls, damaged by sin and knowing evil, just like darkness cannot bear light. Even prayer became difficult for people, since they could no longer see the One to Whom they were turning with their requests.

Chapter Eight

How God Saved Mankind From Sin and Death

Adam and Eve's fall into sin corrupted our minds and wills and brought sickness and death into our bodies. All of us descend from Adam and Eve, who sinned, and so we are all born in a state of sin. Sin, being passed in an unbroken chain from generation to generation, gained power over all people and made them submit to it. All people are sinful, some more and others less. Remember, sin is the breaking of God's will. That is why sin always leads us away from God and towards suffering, sickness, and eternal death. Human beings themselves were no longer able to defeat sin and its consequences in themselves by their own strength. They couldn't heal their minds, wills, and hearts, and couldn't destroy death.

Only God Himself, the Creator of all things, could do that. And He, in His mercy, fulfilled the promise He had given to Adam and Eve and came to our aid by sending to earth His Son, our Savior Jesus Christ.

When the time for salvation had come, the Son of God dwelt within the most-pure Virgin Mary and by the power of the Holy Spirit took on human nature from her. He was born in a supernatural manner "of the Holy Spirit and the Virgin Mary."

The most-holy Mary is called "Virgin" because out of love for God, she made a vow never to get married. The Holy Orthodox Church calls the Virgin Mary the "Theotokos" and honors her more highly than any other created being: not just higher than other human beings, but also higher than the angels, as one who is "more honorable than the Cherubim and more glorious beyond compare than the Seraphim," since she is the mother of the Lord Himself.

> *Something "supernatural" is something outside the normal way the natural world works. Since God established the natural world and its rules, they are subject to His will and He can bend them when He wishes.*

> *Do you recognize these words? They are part of a hymn that we sing both in Church and in our private prayers.*

The Lord Jesus Christ accomplished our salvation through His teaching, His life, and His death and Resurrection. His teaching brings us salvation when we receive it with our whole soul and act according to it, when we try to imitate the life of the Savior with our whole lives. The false words of the Devil that the first created people accepted became the seeds of sin and death in them. Christ's words of truth, when we as Christians receive them diligently, become for us the seeds of holy and immortal life.

We need to believe with all our strength that Christ is our true God and receive the mystery of Holy Baptism, so that we can experience the effect of faith in Christ and truly be saved. If you have read the Gospels, you remember that Jesus Christ received baptism from John the Baptist and commanded all people to be baptized as well for the remission of sins. We'll talk more about Baptism later on.

Chapter Nine

The Annunciation of the Most-Holy Theotokos

Every year, the Church celebrates events from the lives of saints, or people who helped in our salvation, as well as important things that happened during Jesus' time on earth. There are many of those events, and as a result, many feasts. But among them, there are some that are the most important, without which the Lord wouldn't have been able to save mankind from death and sin. Four of the most central of these feasts are Annunciation, Nativity, the Crucifixion, and the Resurrection of Christ.

Notice that without the first of those, Annunciation, our salvation would not have taken place. Our salvation became possible because one girl defeated sin in herself and hated evil to such a degree that she was able to commune with God. She desired the salvation of humanity and wanted to help God so much, that she agreed to serve Him in this truly difficult work. That girl was the Most-Holy Virgin Mary.

The Most-Holy Virgin Mary, the Mother of God, was the daughter of the righteous Joachim and Anna. They were both pious people and were well known, not for their royal lineage, but for their humility and charity. Their whole life was permeated with love for God and for other people. They lived to old age but did not have any children, which made them very sad. But in spite of their old age, they didn't stop asking God to give them a child. They made a vow that if a child was born to them, they would dedicate that child to the service of God.

For their patience, great faith, and love for God and each other, the Lord sent Joachim and Anna a great joy. Near the end of their lives, a daughter was born to them. According to the instructions of an angel of God, she was given the name Mary, which is Hebrew for "Lady" or "Hope."

When the Virgin Mary was three years old and her parents were still alive, they gave their daughter to be raised in the Temple of God. Mary spent her whole childhood there. Zealous and meek, she loved to pray to God more than anything and was obedient to Him in all things. She was very intelligent and hardworking. Everyone loved her very much, and they were surprised that she was so modest and wise beyond her years.

When Mary grew up, she loved God so much that she made a vow never to get married. Her parents had already died by that time, so the priests of the temple where she was raised gave her into the care of a distant relative of hers, a God-fearing old man named Joseph. Mary settled in his house. There, she lived the same modest life that she had in the temple. Her favorite activities were prayer, reading the Holy Scriptures, needlework, and helping the poor. The Lord saw that Mary was more modest and kind than all the other maidens in the world, and that she prayed more fervently than all others, and tried to do God's will in all things. And so, God chose Mary to be the Mother of the Lord Jesus Christ, the Savior of the world.

And so once, when Mary was reading a sacred book, her whole little room was lit up with an unusual light, and an angel of God appeared before her with flowers in his hands and said to her, "Rejoice, holy and good virgin! The Lord is with you! Through your humility, your fervent prayers, and your love for God, you have become worthy of a great mercy. The Holy Spirit will descend upon you and you will give birth to a Son. You shall name him Jesus. He will be great because He is the Son of God, the Savior of the world, and He will save mankind from sin and death."

The Virgin Mary, in her meekness, hadn't expected such happiness and such great honor. She didn't think she was worthy to become the Mother of the Savior. But since she loved God more than anything and was used to being obedient to Him, she humbly answered the angel, "I am the handmaiden of the Lord. Let it be to me as the Lord God wishes."

Then the angel joyfully returned to God. The foundation of the salvation of mankind had been laid.

Through her humble obedience to the will of God, the Most-Holy Virgin Mary became the complete opposite of Eve, fixing and making amends for Eve's sin.

All of this is found in the first chapter of the Gospel of Luke.

This good news that was "announced" to the Virgin Mary (which is why the feast is called the "Annunciation") is celebrated in the Orthodox Church on March 25th—nine months ahead of Christmas, when we celebrate Jesus' birth, the same amount of time it takes for a baby to be born. The feast of the Annunciation is one of the biggest feasts in the Church year, because we celebrate the good news that God has begun to free mankind from sin and eternal death.

Chapter Ten

The Nativity of Jesus Christ (Christmas)

One day, righteous Joseph and holy Mary set out from the city of Nazareth, where they lived, for the city of Bethlehem. At that time, many people were gathering there because of a census, and so all of the houses and even all of the smallest huts were full.

What could they do? Joseph and Mary were exhausted and needed to rest. When they couldn't find a place to stay, either in a house or in an inn, they stayed outside the city in a cave where shepherds would stay with their flocks when the weather was bad, although since in that country, there is no winter, they more often slept in the fields by night. That night was particularly bright and warm and so this cave, which had been dug into the side of a mountain, was empty.

That night in the cave, the Most-Holy Virgin Mary gave birth to an Infant, the Son of God, Christ, the Savior of the world. She swaddled the Divine Child and placed Him in a manger, a feeding trough for animals. Jesus, the Son of God, was lying in the manger and the shepherds were spending the night in the field. Suddenly, a radiant, shining angel appeared to the shepherds like a bolt of lightning. The shepherds were scared, but the angel spoke to them kindly, saying, "Do not be afraid, I bring you glad tidings of great joy! Go to your cave and there you will see a small Child, who is Jesus, the Son of God, the Savior of the world."

The angel had just disappeared when the shepherds suddenly heard wondrous sounds coming from Heaven, as beautiful as the music of a great organ. Whole choirs of angels had come down from Heaven to greet the Infant Jesus, their King and Creator. All of the angels sang and rejoiced that the loving Lord had sent His son to earth to redeem all humanity and open for them the way to His Heavenly Kingdom.

When the angels had left, the shepherds set out for the cave. When they saw the Divine Child, they bowed down and worshiped Him.

By God's command, above the cave where Jesus Christ was born, an unusually large and beautiful star was shining. Many people saw it in other countries, even countries that were far away. Rich, learned men, and wise men, the Magi, came from far Eastern countries to the cave to worship Him. They spent their time observing and studying the stars. In those days people believed that when a great person was born, a new star would appear in the sky. Many people believed prophecies that a great King and Savior was supposed to be born into the world. They were expecting a new star to appear when that great King was born. The Magi were pious people and the Lord, in His mercy, gave them a sign – a new, unusual star appeared in the sky. When they saw that star, the Magi understood immediately that the long-awaited King had been born. They set out to follow where the star would lead them. When they got to Bethlehem, they saw that the star had come to rest over a certain house where Joseph and the Virgin Mary had moved to from the cave with the Child; it was that long a journey for the Magi to get there. The Magi entered the house and saw the Infant Jesus with His Mother. They bowed down and worshiped Him and gave Him gifts of gold, frankincense, and myrrh (a precious, fragrant substance).

The story of Christ's nativity is found in the second chapter of the Gospel of Luke.

By their gifts, the Magi showed that the newborn Child was King, and God, and man. They brought Him gold because He is King, frankincense because He is God (since incense is used in divine worship), and myrrh because He is a man who was going to die (since at the time, the dead were anointed with sweet-smelling ointments, which often had myrrh in them).

They showed honor to the Infant as God and King of Kings. Tradition has preserved for us the names of the Magi, who later became Christians: Melchior, Gaspar, and Balthasar.

The holy Orthodox Church celebrates the Nativity of our Lord Jesus Christ on December 25th. We prepare ourselves for this great feast by fasting for forty days, which is called the Nativity Fast. On Christmas Eve, according to the Church Typikon, we only eat boiled grains with honey and that only in the evening, after the appearance of the first star.

Chapter Eleven

Christic is Risen!

In the Orthodox Church, the glorious Resurrection of Christ is celebrated as the greatest of all feasts, since it was by His resurrection from the dead, after His crucifixion and death, that Christ accomplished something unheard of. He conquered death which mankind had been unable to overcome.

The bright Resurrection of Christ is the feast of feasts and festival of festivals. It is so important, that it is outside the twelve other Great Feasts, superior to all of them. If Christ had not risen from the dead, not only would there not be Christianity, but also faith in God, in the power of goodness and in righteousness would be undermined, and life would lose its meaning. The truth of the Resurrection of the Savior is found in the fact that it was the God-man who rose from the dead. He raised the human flesh that He had taken on Himself and transfigured human nature into a nature that is spiritual and divine, destined for eternal life with God. That is what the Savior's victory over death means for the whole human race.

The feast of Christ's Resurrection is also called

"Pascha," from the Hebrew word for "Passover," since it is the day when we passed over from death to life and from earth to heaven. The feast of Pascha lasts for a whole week (seven days) and the divine services in Church are served in a special way, more solemnly than at any other feast or day. On the first day of the feast, Matins begins at midnight. Before the beginning of Matins, the clergy, dressed in bright clothing, make a procession around the church with the faithful, holding lit candles, a cross, and icons, while the bells ring. This reminds us of the holy Myrrhbearing Women who went early in the morning to the grave of the Savior. During the procession, everyone sings "Thy Resurrection, O Christ our Savior, the angels in heaven sing. Make us also on earth worthy to glorify Thee in purity of heart." Sometimes they also sing the Trisagion hymn, "Holy God, Holy Mighty, Holy Immortal, have mercy on us," in a joyful tone. The exclamation at the beginning of Matins is done in front of the Church doors, and then the Paschal Troparion, "Christ is risen from the dead..." is sung over and over again as the people enter the Church. All week, the services are served with the Holy Doors on the iconostasis open, as a sign that the doors to the Kingdom of God have now been opened by Christ's resurrection. Every day of this feast, we greet each other with a brotherly kiss and with the words, "Christ is risen!" and answer with the words, "Truly He is risen!" We kiss each other three times and exchange painted red eggs, which serve as a symbol of the new, blessed life that shone forth from the Savior's grave. All week long, when the church bells are rung, all of them are rung together.

In addition, we commemorate the day of Christ's resurrection every week, on Sunday.

The Cross

People who aren't familiar with Christ might think that it's strange that the Cross is so important to us as Christians, since it is an instrument of death. However, the death of Christ is life-bearing. Through His Crucifixion and death, Christ destroyed the power of death and any reason we have to be afraid. On the Cross, Christ took on Himself our sin, our condemnation, and our death and poured out into us, in exchange, His divine life and the promise of the Resurrection. For that reason, the Cross is a sign of victory, not defeat, and we make the sign of the Cross to remind ourselves of Christ's voluntary sacrifice for our salvation.

Chapter Twelve

Hades

Because of Adam and Eve's horrible choice, death, sin, and illness permeated the world that God had created. Death is the separation of soul and body. In death, we are split into the parts that we were made out of and our bodies decay. Our souls, when separated from our bodies, were supposed to go to Hades, the place where Satan and his fallen angels (the demons) abide since, because of our sins, our souls could no longer commune with God and had submitted themselves to Satan.

Sins are actions that go against God's will, and that bring evil and death with themselves. Sin is hatred, enmity, envy, pride and all the consequences of those feelings. Adam and Evil did not do those kinds of things until they had gone against God's will. But once they had gone against His will, they no longer had the strength to keep from doing other evil deeds.

Sickness is when the human body breaks down as a result of the sins of the soul. The soul lost its power over the body and so it lost God's help and broke its communion with God. The body, without the soul guiding it and without God's life-giving help, began to fall apart.

And so, through sin, death and sickness entered the world.

Until the saving coming and resurrection of the Lord Jesus Christ, all souls, as we already said, went to Hades after death when they were separated from their bodies.

What exactly is Hades and where is it?

Hades is a place removed from God's presence, where God sent Satan and the other fallen angels. Often people say that Hades is located under the ground but we shouldn't understand that literally. People say that to express how far Hades is from Heaven, where God and His angels abide. We don't know how to express where Hades or the Kingdom of Heaven are. In this life, we can only see them with spiritual eyes, with our soul, if God allows it.

Souls in Hades are tormented because they can no longer do what they were used to doing during their lives – eat, drink, insult others, boast, buy things, have fun, and many other things. They are also tormented because they cannot commune with God and by the fact that they themselves, voluntarily lived their lives in a way that led them to Hades.

God wants to help those souls, too, but the souls themselves, having spent their whole lives doing evil and not knowing God, can no longer accept His help and feel His love. And so the doors of Hades are locked from the inside.

Until the coming of Christ, the souls of the righteous also went to Hades. However, there they suffered not from their own malice and spite, but rather from being separated from God and seeing the suffering of sinners. After the Crucifixion, Christ descended to Hades and led the souls of the righteous to Paradise. From that time on, only the souls of the unrighteous who did not love others go to Hades. I am sure none of us would like to go there!

Chapter Thirteen

Paradise

Paradise is the Kingdom of Heaven, where the Lord shows Himself most clearly, and where the good angels and the souls of the righteous live.

Many people have tried to describe what is waiting for us in Heaven, how wonderful it is, but no one has been able to do it. The Apostle Paul, whom the Lord allowed to see Paradise while still alive, said as much when he said about what he saw that "man shall not utter" it.

All that we can say about Paradise is that there, every person will finally get to learn and experience what he was created for. Each of us will feel the force of Divine love and know true happiness. God has prepared for each of us what we need and what He created each of us for. Just like a key fits a lock because it was made for it, so we each fit Paradise. We will be in joyful communion with each other and with God. God will find a task for each of us that gives meaning to eternal life. As we fulfill that task, we will ascend further into limitless joy and continually draw closer to God. Since God is infinite, that means that our joy will also be infinite, doesn't it?

Chapter Fourteen

The Church

You have probably heard the word "Church" more than once without really knowing what it means. The word for "Church" in Greek, "Ecclesia," means "an assembly." This word can also mean the house of the Lord, the place where we can commune with God, where He helps us. Christians, those people who believe in Christ, understand the word Church to mean the community of people who believe in God, the Holy Trinity, and in Jesus Christ, the Son of God, who came to save us from sin and eternal death, and who gave us the forgiveness and remission of sins, eternal life, and the inheritance of the Kingdom of Heaven. The Lord established the Church on the fiftieth day after His resurrection. He commanded His apostles to gather in one room and then the Holy Spirit – the third Person of the Holy Trinity – descended on them. He taught the apostles everything that Christians need to know and formed them into the Church. The apostles taught others to believe in Christ and in the Most-Holy Trinity, and so faith in Him and His Church spread throughout the world.

This means that the Church is the assembly

of those who believe in Christ, including both those who are alive and those who are physically dead (that is, whose souls have been separated from their bodies but who remain in communion with God in Heaven). When we say "in Heaven," we mean in the Kingdom of Heaven, in Paradise.

The word church also means the Lord's house, the temple, the place where we commune with God. In other words, a Christian is a participant in the Assembly of the Faithful – the Church – and also goes to a church, the place where that Assembly gathers.

To help Christians and to strengthen their faith, the Lord God, the Holy Trinity, created the Holy Mysteries, which are also called Sacraments. In the Church, "Mysteries" don't mean detective stories. They are called "Mysteries" because understanding them completely is beyond human ability and only possible for God. The Holy Mysteries are miraculous divine acts, through which human beings can receive healing from eternal death and sickness

When we write, we capitalize "Church" for the Assembly of the Faithful, the Church as a whole, but we do not capitalize "church" as in "church building," unless it is part of the name of a specific building, such as "St. Paul's Church." This is because a building can be destroyed or burnt down, but the Church, the Assembly of the Faithful, is eternal.

and the forgiveness of their sins. Through the Holy Mysteries, we also receive the gift of eternal life and God's help (which we call grace) in all good deeds. There is also the Mystery of Ordination, where Divine Grace is given to make someone into a priest or deacon, and the Mystery of Marriage, or "Crowning," where the Lord gives grace and His blessing to young men and women who love each other and want to start a family.

All together, there are seven Mysteries – Baptism, Chrismation, Communion, Confession, Unction, Crowning, and Ordination. Each of these mysteries gives us the divine help, or grace, that we need. And all of these mysteries find their fulfillment only in the Orthodox Church.

Do you see what a complicated and important concept the Church is?

Chapter Fifteen

The Mystery of Holy Baptism

We already know that each of us is born into the world with a nature that has been twisted by sin. We inherit from Adam and Eve the consequences of the sin they committed: sickness, death, and a desire to do evil. No one can be freed from these consequences of sin without God's help. That is why the Lord gave us the Mystery of Holy Baptism to heal our damaged nature. In this Mystery, we are submerged in water three times and renounce Satan and all fellowship with him. We also confess our faith in the Holy Trinity and in Jesus Christ, the Son of God, and receive His saving sacrifice for us. The Holy Spirit works through the water that we see with our eyes and feel with our body, invisibly changing and healing the defects in our human nature that we were born with. The Holy Spirit also makes us able to have communion with God in the other Mysteries and delivers us from the sins that we ourselves have committed. In Baptism, we are born again, with a healed nature and sins that have been forgiven. Infants that are baptized are still given a renewed nature, even if they haven't committed any personal sins yet.

Without Holy Baptism, we cannot become members of the Church or receive the other Mysteries. If we haven't been baptized, then we haven't been born into eternal life or healed from eternal death.

Chapter Sixteen

The Mystery of the Eucharist (Holy Communion)

There are many adults who still do not understand why we need to go to Church. "If God knows everything and can be everywhere, then I can commune with Him anywhere. Why do I have to go to Church and stand through the divine services there?" they say. But they talk like that because they don't understand.

Of course, God hears us everywhere. But do we hear Him everywhere? And does He give us His most precious gift to mankind, the Holy Gifts, the Body and Blood of Christ that we read about in the Gospel, everywhere?

You see, it is only in the temple, only during the Liturgy that the most amazing and saving Mystery takes place, when bread and wine are transformed into the Body and Blood of Christ, and then distributed to Christians to give life to their souls and bodies, and to give them strength to do battle against sickness and have victory over sin and death.

All of you have probably read fairy tales about a magic water of life that can raise the dead. The Lord has given those who believe in Him a much more powerful Gift that is able to defeat the death in us and help us become God's friends and the heirs of His Heavenly Kingdom.

And so the most important divine service, the most important moment in our lives, our true feast, is called the Eucharist. "Eucharist" means "thanksgiving." Since the Lord has given us the gift of this life-creating Mystery, we give thanks to Him during the divine service.

The bread and wine are only transformed into the true Body and Blood of Christ, the Son of God, through the prayer of a priest. No one except God knows how this happens. When we partake of the Holy Gifts, we become communicants of Christ and participate in eternal life, which God gives us through them. That is why this Mystery is called "Communion." In order for us to call ourselves Christians and inherit the Kingdom of

Heaven and eternal life, we must be baptized in the Church and partake in the Eucharist.

It is a great mystery how the Lord, at the prayers of His priest, changes the bread and wine into the Body and Blood of Christ, the Holy Gifts. It is an even greater mystery and even harder to understand how the Holy Gifts work in us. But all who believe in Christ and who want to fulfill His commandments can feel them at work in themselves. That is why we go to Church, to taste the Holy Gifts and to give thanks to God for this wonderful and saving gift that He gives us human beings.

Now you know why we should go to Church and why we need the Church to call ourselves Christians. We cannot be Christians without these saving gifts (John 6:53).

Chapter Seventeen

The Mystery of Repentance (Confession)

The Eucharist is vital to our lives as Christians, both here on earth and in Eternity, but if we want to receive the Holy Gifts from God and if we want them to be a help to us, we should cleanse our hearts and consciences from all evil deeds. Otherwise, the Lord cannot heal us from sin and eternal death.

But how can we cleanse our consciences? For this, the Lord has given us another saving Mystery: the Mystery of Repentance, or Holy Confession.

Repentance is sincere remorse for our bad deeds, words, and thoughts, and Confession is when we tell a priest about our sins. Why can't we just ask God to forgive us? Why do we need a priest? Of course, not only can we ask God for forgiveness, but we should do so as soon as we've done something wrong. But how can we know that we have received that forgiveness? After all, we can't see forgiveness with our eyes or touch it with our hands. Of course, the Lord will cleanse our consciences and we will feel relief. But God has given the priest authority to remit sins in a visible way so that no one, not even the demons, can reproach us for the sins we have committed. That takes place in Confession.

We come to Church and approach the priest who is hearing confessions and tell him about the things that we have done that our conscience reproaches us for. Then, we bow our head and the priest covers our head with his epitrachelion (ep-ee-truh-HEL-ee-own), a special piece of his vestments (sometimes also called a "stole"), and then says a prayer in which, by the power given to him by God, he looses and forgives us of our sins that we have confessed.

If we hide something shameful that we've done and don't repent, then we aren't forgiven that sin in Confession. If we forget something, though, then we can mention it the next time we got to Confession.

As soon we go to Confession and tell God our sins – such as not telling the truth, being rude or disobedient, and whatever else we have done – our conscience is cleansed and we can go forward to receive Communion without condemnation. But if we go as we are, with a conscience that hasn't been washed and a soul that is stained with sins, then the Holy Gifts do not heal us and give us life. Rather, we receive them to our condemnation. The living water of salvation becomes the water of judgment.

Chapter Eighteen

The Ten Commandments

Probably at some point when you're doing something wrong, you've heard someone tell you, "Don't do that. It's a sin!" As we've already talked about, sin is lawlessness. But what does that look like in our daily lives? We all know, of course, how easy it is to break a toy or some other object if you don't take care of it, if you throw it on the floor or hit it. But as human beings, we become "b r o k e n" when, in the course of our lives, we break the Law of God that God has given us so that our souls can escape death and come to know God.

In the Old Testament, we read about how the people of Israel, God's chosen people, were held as slaves in Egypt. God chose His servant Moses to lead the people out of slavery. Once they had escaped Egypt, He led Moses up to the top of Mt. Sinai and gave him the Ten Commandments. St. Paul says that when we sin, we are slaves to sin. Following God's will brings us to true freedom.

The commandments, which were given to the prophet Moses thousands of years ago on Mount Sinai, are the very same laws that we need to know for the life of our soul. Here they are:

1. Honor God above all things

This means that we should look to God (Who is, of course, personal and not some kind of abstract "force" like in Star Wars) as the One who means more to us than anything in the world. We never want to offend or sadden those that we love. Rather, we try to do what we can to bring joy and gladness to those that we value. And so, if you honor and love God above all things, that means that you want God to always be with you and want Him to always find joy in you.

No one is more perfect, more kind, more wonderful, or more loving than God. Nothing and no one is better than He is. He is perfection itself. And if you speak with Him in prayer, you will certainly be able to understand that He will help you. But if you don't want to pray to Him, then how can He show you His love?

2. Do not worship idols

Many things can fill this role – old friends, computer games, and even money. We are worshiping idols whenever we make a dream, a goal, a person, or anything else more important than anything else in our lives. For example, if we dream about getting rich and famous, or if convincing our parents to let us play on the computer is the most important thing to us, then those

> *Even though God had just freed them from slavery to the Egyptians, the people of Israel quickly turned to idols. While Moses was up on Mt. Sinai, the people melted their jewelry to make a calf out of gold and began to worship it instead of God. Only the true God, however, can save us and give us eternal life.*

things are idols for us. There are many dreams and pleasures in life that aren't good or bad in and of themselves. But not everything that is not bad is good for the health of our souls and not everything leads to our happiness.

3. Do not offend God by using His name in vain

We offend God when we openly oppose His commandments and do not love His creation, both people and nature. We offend God when we are rude and profane and when we ruin and break everything that He has made, people, animals, plants, etc. We offend God when in response to Him having created us, we hate ourselves and the world around us, not using the talents that He has given us.

4. Remember the Sabbath and keep it holy

Since we usually spend our life chasing after the pleasures of this world, this commandment is needed so that we can pause what we're doing and remember what is waiting for us – eternal life. And how do we remember that? The best way is by talking with God in prayer and being joined to Him in Holy Communion. That is why the Church has set aside one day a week, Sunday, as a holy day. On Sunday, Christians should try to avoid working for money and entertainment. On this day, we should try to spend at least a little time alone, away from our loved ones, and think about our relationship with God and with our neighbors.

5. Honor your father and mother

We should remember that God gave us the gift of life through our parents, and so we should approach them with thankfulness and try to be obedient and not rude to them. When we honor our parents, we should feel compassion towards them. Without compassion, love is impossible. Have compassion and honor the people who gave up their health, their peace, and their time for your sake. It doesn't matter how much time they spent with you. Whether it was a lot of time or a little, it was still a sacrifice. Remember that you also aren't always able to give your whole attention to the well-being of your friends and relatives.

6. Do not kill

This commandment means more than just killing. We can "kill" someone by insults, betrayal, and disdain. And so before we say something or try to prove ourselves to others (friends, parents, adults) we should stop and think and make sure that our behavior isn't hurting or offending anyone. That applies also to animals and nature. We do not have the right to hurt or torment animals, to tear down trees, to litter, to dirty the world around ourselves. The Lord gave us this world for life, not for us to break and disfigure everything it.

7. Do not commit adultery

That means "Do not be unfaithful to God and yourself." Unfaithfulness in the spiritual sense means for us to stray from the right path, to betray God, ourselves, and our calling. That is why the prophet, when talking

Adultery is also when people whom God has joined together in marriage do not respect the sacredness of their bond with each other in Christ.

about the Israelites who worshiped pagan gods and broke the commandments, says that they have "committed adultery in their ways."

8. Do not steal

Stealing is when we take something that isn't ours, that we haven't earned by our own work. But stealing is more than just taking something. For example, sneaking in somewhere without paying when there's an entry fee is also a form of stealing.

9. Do not lie

Everyone knows that it isn't good to lie. For some reason, though, we often don't pay any special attention to it and stretch the truth in both big and little ways. When we get used to lying, it ruins us on the inside in the same way that rust ruins metal and worms ruin apples. A liar, even if he seems pleasant on the outside, is rotten on the inside because he can't be relied on for anything that is important.

10. Do not covet

We covet when we want to take for ourselves what we haven't earned by our own righteousness, our own talents, or our own work – things that rightfully belong to others. For some reason, we often think that the opposite deserve things that others have. That is envy.

Sin is our refusal to live according to these spiritual laws, and so sin already contains within it a punishment. When we sin, we twist and break the marvelous gift that God has given us, our soul.

Chapter Nineteen

The Beatitudes

In addition to the Ten Commandments that forbid us from doing evil, the Lord has also left with us other commandments called the Beatitudes, which do the opposite and

The Beatitudes are found in the fifth chapter of the Gospel of Matthew.

tell us what we should do, how to live a blessed, joyful life and how to inherit from God eternal life and the Kingdom of Heaven.

1. Blessed are the poor in spirit for theirs is the Kingdom of Heaven

Poverty in spirit is when we recognize that everything that we have – our life, our health, our strength, our abilities, our knowledge, and our possessions – all of it is a gift from God. When we know this and thank God for His gifts, we recognize our poverty before God. If we receive all of God's gifts with thanksgiving, the Lord has even more gifts to give us. We are truly blessed when we learn to receive God's gifts with thanksgiving!

All of us, at one time or another, have been unhappy about something. Maybe it was a toy, food, the color of our eyes, our parents' rules, sickness, physical weakness, or something like that. There are too many things to list. But here's the thing: everything that we have and ever will have, all of it is a gift from the Lord, that He has given us either directly or through the people close to us: parents, relatives, etc. If, when we look at these gifts, we are dissatisfied and turn up our nose, why would anyone want to give us more gifts? When you give someone a gift, no one likes a sour look or a rude word in return. And if instead of giving thanks, we point at the people around us and say, "Why does he have that and I don't?" then we're not only ungrateful, but also envious. And then we'll never be able to see God's blessings. Even a gift that seems unpleasant or makes our earthly lives difficult can be a way to become closer to God.

For in order for us to become like God intended us to be, we have to stop comparing ourselves with others and learn to give thanks to God for what we have. Only then will the Lord help us to become someone great, to become better. That is the recipe for blessedness that the Lord has given us.

2. Blessed are those who weep for they shall be comforted

That's a very strange way to be happy, isn't it? But we've already heard about this kind of blessedness when we talked about Confession. Yes, Confession is this same path to blessedness. If we repent of our bad deeds to the point of tears, if more than anything else, we want to correct the evil that we have done, then that is our path to happiness. Weeping and repentance for our bad actions, our desire to repair what we have done: that is the second path that leads to blessedness.

If you also feel pity for those around you who are suffering, people, animals, plants... Then you can ask the Lord on their behalf and then that prayer will be added to your repentance. Prayer is a weapon that changes the world and conquers evil. And the Lord promises you that you will be comforted. Evil will be conquered, sin will be washed away by repentance, and you yourself will be glorified.

3. Blessed are the meek, for they shall inherit the Earth

How can this be? On TV, in games, and even in life itself, it seems like the winners are always those who are stronger, more agile, and smarter.

Yes, it seems that way. But even the biggest victories only last until someone stronger comes along. And even that stronger person will face justice in death.

But in this Beatitude, the Lord promises us that we will inherit the Earth! And doesn't that mean that in that case, no one will ever be able to take away our victory?

For whoever is victorious in the battle against evil will never have that victory taken away. That victory is eternal. But you can't defeat evil by fighting against it with weapons. You cannot conquer evil with evil, force with force, and cunning with cunning. The Lord instructs us to use a different sort of weapon, one that cannot be overcome – meekness.

Meekness is when the human soul is filled with love and peace. When we are meek, our soul firmly hopes in God and believes that with the Lord, all things are possible. Meekness is the absence of irritation, indignation (being offended), and malice (bad intent). When we are meek, we no longer want to answer a blow with a stronger blow and an insult with a worse insult. Meekness is when we allow God to act in us and through us. If we allow God to do that, the Lord will be victorious in our hearts and give us our inheritance. And our inheritance is the world which He has created, the Earth.

4. Blessed are those who hunger and thirst after righteousness for they shall be filled

This commandment also might seem strange at first glance. Of course, when people are hungry, they are satisfied when they eat their fill; and when they are thirsty, they are satisfied when they have a good drink of water. But what does it mean to "hunger and thirst after righteousness" and how will they be satisfied if righteousness is not bread or meat, not water or milk or juice; when you can't eat it or drink it? It turns out that those who "hunger and thirst after righteousness" are those people who desire righteousness as strongly as someone who is starving and tormented by thirst wants to eat and drink.

But what is this "righteousness"? Is it when we seek justice when someone has wronged us? Is righteousness when we always tell the truth? Not exactly. There are many people in the world and if you were to ask each of them, they would each have a different opinion about what righteousness is. Each of us likes to think that what we like or what is convenient for us is what is just. But the righteousness of God is the same for everyone and comes from the Lord who knows all of our hardships and desires. Eternal righteousness is peace between man and God. It is our justification before Him. Jesus Christ Himself is the righteousness that is eternal, as He said about Himself, "I am the way, the truth, and the life" (John 14:6). That means that those who want to be with Jesus Christ forever and do His will, to be kind to others and love them, are the ones who will be truly happy.

The Lord promises those people who desire righteousness with all their hearts that they will be filled. Of course, they will be filled spiritually. When we desire righteousness and live honestly, according to the truth, without offending God, our souls will always be at peace and our consciences will always be calm. This spiritual fullness is somewhat like when our bodies are filled and comforted when we are hungry and tired, and then eat our fill and peace, joy, and warmth fill our whole being. But internal, spiritual peace is much more important and necessary for us – that peace that is found in a tranquil conscience, in justification and mercy, in spiritual peace in God. And we will "be filled" because the Lord will fill our souls with peace and joy, and our hearts will no longer have room for bitterness or offense. What is more, the Lord will give those who start to fulfill His commandments the strength to fulfill them, so that with each good deed, it will be easier and easier, and more and more joyful.

5. Blessed are the merciful for they shall receive mercy

The merciful are those who pity anyone who falls into misfortune with their whole heart. Those who are merciful, when they see someone else doing something wrong, don't say to them, "You are wicked! You deserve what's happening to you and more! God will punish you!" Rather, they sigh and remember the wrongs that they have done and think, "Lord, forgive all of us the evil that we do."

There are many ways to show mercy. We can and should show mercy by actively helping anyone who is in need – by feeding the hungry, clothing the poor, visiting and comforting the sick, and protecting the weak. There are thousands of good deeds that we can do out of mercy! We don't even need to travel very far. You can feel pity for your parents and help them with chores, even ones you are not required to do. That is also mercy.

Mercy can sometimes be invisible to the eye but very necessary for the soul. We can comfort those who are weeping, not insult those who insult us, not get revenge, pray for those who are having a difficult time, give a kind piece of advice, teach someone without faith to believe in God, and pray for those who have died and who can no longer pray for themselves...

In short, when we have pity on the people

around us, the Lord also will have pity on us. That is His promise to us.

6. Blessed are the pure in heart for they shall see God

How can we see God in this life if it is impossible to see Him? But we already talked about how we can see God, not with our eyes, but with our heart and soul. In order for that to happen, our souls have to learn to see, to gain their sight. Just as we clean our windows if we want to have a better look at what's going on outside, in the same way, if we want to see the spiritual world, to see God, we need to wash our spiritual eyes, the eyes of our heart. Of course we should understand both "eyes" and "heart" allegorically, as powers and properties of the soul. Just like the heart is the most important organ in our body, in the same way the soul has a center, out of which our thoughts and desires flow. For simplicity, that was also given the name of "heart."

This means that the pure in heart are those people who not only don't commit wicked acts, but for whom even the thought of evil is distasteful. A pure heart is a heart that is free from hatred, pride, and cruelty.

It takes a lot of work to achieve purity of heart. We begin with prayer to God, asking for

His help, and then continue our battle with our harmful and evil desires. For example, you might feel like skipping class at school, but then you overcome that desire and go to school. You want to be rude, and then you overcome your desire to do something wrong and are polite. The same thing applies in everything, in food, games, housework...

But since communion with God is mankind's greatest joy, then those whom God decides to commune with, those who have communion with Him, will be truly happy.

However, when our hearts are hardened and coarse, then God's love and care for us becomes the biggest torment, because we feel shame and the gnawing of our consciences. That is why those whose hearts have not been cleansed are not only unable to see God, but do not even desire to.

7. Blessed are the peacemakers for they shall be called the sons of God

We call those who try to live in peace and friendship with everyone in the world around them "peacemakers." People who try to reconcile those who have quarreled and who pray to God to reconcile them are also called "peacemakers."

What exactly is "peace," and why is it so precious to God that the Lord pointed to peacemaking as a special path that leads to Him?

We know what it is to experience peace. Peace of the soul is when all of our soul's faculties are in harmony and friendship with each other. In Greek there is a word, "sophrosyne," which means "whole minded," that describes what it is like when there is no war in our soul, no division, but only peace. Our mind is whole and undivided and so it becomes wise and understands the meaning of all things.

We talked earlier about the Holy Trinity and about how one of the chief characteristics of God the Trinity is the harmony and peace that reign among God the Father, the Son, and the Holy Spirit. It is difficult for us even to imagine that harmony. But let's take a moment and try to understand it by looking at the example of the great Russian saint, Venerable Sergius of Radonezh. His whole life, St. Sergius strove to overcome sin in his soul. And when he finally achieved that and cleansed his heart, he beheld God, like the Lord promised in this Beatitude. When he beheld God, he was able to perceive the peace, love, and harmony that God has in Himself. Then, St. Sergius passed all of that on to a great and holy iconographer, St. Andrei Rublev. St. Andrei then worked hard on his own soul and through prayer and the cleansing of his heart, he was able to convey that divine blessedness through paint, as much as that is possible. Now, we can see and understand the beauty of that spiritual peace by looking at St. Andrei's famous icon of the

Holy Trinity. When we look at the faces of the three Angels, we can see with our own eyes the beauty of those who have attained peace of soul and whom the Lord calls His children.

Peacemakers, those who have overcome discord in themselves, are able to overcome discord and hatred in the whole world, to extinguish wars and bring joy. In doing that, they become like God, and obtain joy and happiness.

8. Blessed are those who are persecuted for righteousness, for theirs is the Kingdom of Heaven

Often we say that we believe in something, but when we are asked about our faith, we respond in different ways. We might feel embarrassed and not stick to what we said, or on the other hand, we might defend and speak up for our faith.

Only a few decades ago in the Soviet Union, the Orthodox Church and even faith in Christ were forbidden. Priests were sent to prison and executed; faithful Christians were laughed at and expelled from school, fired from their jobs, and kicked out of their houses. And if Christians had not believed that the Lord is the True God and that He is always with us and helps us, they would not have had the firmness and courage to bear the unrighteousness and injustice that the unbelievers put them through.

But faith by itself is not enough. In order to overcome the greatest difficulties that face us and not be bitter or angry with those who hurt us, we need to have love in our hearts as well. We need to love the Lord Jesus Christ more than anything in the world. Then, He will always be with us and will be able to help us. But how can we love God when we cannot see Him?

In order to do that, like it says in the Gospel, we need to learn to love the people around us. We start, of course, with our friends, our parents, our siblings, our grandparents, our teachers; then, from there, even the people, for example, who are riding in the same bus as us. But you might say that that is impossible. Loving our grandparents is one thing, but how can we love some stranger? Here is how. If you want to love someone, do good to them. Give up your seat to them, smile in response to a frown, pray for them... There are so many little things that we can do – wash the dishes, take out the garbage, help someone carry their bags, be kind when someone is rude – and all of those things build up in our heart like money in a piggy-bank. It is up to you whether the piggy-bank of your soul will be filled with love, kindness, and beauty, or whether it will be filled with the blackness of malice and ungratefulness.

What then of those "who are persecuted for righteousness sake"? Yes, it is true. Those who do evil cannot stand those who do good. For someone who does evil, a good person is like a living accusation and reproach against them. Because of that, throughout all of history, the followers of Christ, who bring goodness and light into the world, have been persecuted by those who cannot stand goodness and light. But we know that our true homeland is in the Kingdom of God and so we are ready to suffer for the sake of Christ.

9. Blessed are you when people insult you, persecute you and falsely say all kinds of evil against you because of me. Rejoice and be glad, because great is your reward in heaven

This last Beatitude strengthens the previous one and explains it at the same time—for it is not enough to tell the truth. We need to be able to tell the difference between truth and righteousness and a mistake that we happen to have believed in. The Lord has given us a marvelous way to test anything to see if it is true and righteous: the Commandments and Christ Himself. Yes, the Lord Jesus Christ, true God and true Man, is Himself the truest standard for measuring truth and righteousness. The Lord Jesus Christ is Truth itself. We can judge everything we do in life by looking at the words of Christ, His life, His teaching, and, of course, by praying to Him. We can always say to

Him, "Lord, please help me to decide what I should do," and the Lord will give us understanding. We can turn to Him and say, "Lord, may everything work out according to Thy will," and then the Lord will work everything out in the best possible way. But the best possible way is not always pleasant. This Beatitude reminds us of that.

Very often it happens that the thing that we really need is not something that we want to do or have. For example, what children would want to get healthy vitamins for their birthdays instead of a bicycle, or notebooks for school instead of skates and a music player? You do not often meet children like that! Our whole life is like that. The Lord knows everything about us and wants to give us what we really need the most – salvation and eternal life. The path that leads to these treasures is not easy. It is long and filled with dangers. Just like people who are looking for hidden treasure are ready to bear rain, cold, hunger, and fear for its sake, so also we who are looking for the treasures of Heaven should be prepared.

This Beatitude also tells us that at every moment in our life, no matter what threatens us, we should be ready to answer when someone asks us about our faith. We should say, "I believe in the Most-Holy Trinity and confess that Christ is our true God and the true Son of God." The Symbol of Faith, the Nicene Creed, gives more details about what we believe. We should know it by heart. As

Christians, we pray it at Church during every Liturgy.

This last Beatitude reminds us of the trials that we should expect to face and that we should be ready to face them for the name of Christ.

Remember that while the way may be difficult, our return to our Father's House, the Kingdom of Heaven, will be glorious!

Chapter Twenty

Prayer

God loves His creation. He loves each of us. Just like we can turn to our earthly father or mother, at any time, we can turn to God, our Heavenly Father. And when we turn to Him, that is called "prayer."

That means that prayer is our way of conversing or talking with God. We need prayer just like we need air and food. Everything that we have is from God; nothing is our own. Our life, our abilities, our health, our food, and everything else is given to us by God. In Russian, there is a saying: "Without God, we cannot even make it to the threshold."

Thus, equally in joy, in sorrow, and in need, we should turn to God in prayer. And the Lord is very good and merciful to us. If we turn to Him with a pure heart, with love and zeal, and tell Him what we need, He will certainly fulfill our desire and give us what we need. Sometimes this is not what we want, but it is always what we need. To do this, we need to rely completely on His holy will and wait patiently, because only He knows what we need and when we need it, and what is helpful for us and what is harmful.

When we do not turn to God in prayer, we harm ourselves because then we have no one whom we can expect help from.

Without prayer, we stop loving God, we forget about Him, and we do not fulfill our purpose on earth, which is a sin.

The different kinds of prayer

If we and our loved ones are healthy and prosperous, if we have a place to live, clothing to wear, and food to eat, then we should of course give thanks to God. Those prayers are called prayers of praise and thanksgiving.

If we go through some kind of tragedy, if we are sick or in need, then we turn to God for help. Those prayers are called prayers of supplication. "Supplication" means "asking for help."

And if we have done something evil, if we have sinned and are guilty before God, then we ask for His forgiveness. Those prayers are called prayers of repentance.

Since we often do things that are wrong, before we ask Him for anything, the right thing for us to do (and the polite thing) is for us first to repent before we make our requests to God. And so we always put prayers of repentance ahead of prayers of supplication.

How to pray

If we want God to help us, we should first forgive those who have offended us and make peace with those whom we ourselves have offended.

Of course, God always hears our supplications. More than that, He even knows our desires that we do not say anything about since He is omniscient. But when we are speaking with God in prayer, if we fidget and get distracted and just want to get our prayers over as soon as possible, we are being rude to the One Who created us. God is not pleased with that sort of prayer. Think about it. Are you happy when you ask your mom or dad for something and they turn away from you to watch TV or talk on the phone?

And so if we want our prayers and supplications to be heard, if we want them to be beneficial and to bring us joy, we should approach prayer as the most important thing that we have to do in our life. Prayer is the most important thing we have to do. It is only through prayer that we can change ourselves and the world around us for the better.

When and where to pray

We can pray to God anywhere, since God is present everywhere. He is with us at home, at Church, as we go on our way. As Christians, we have an obligation to pray to God every day, in the morning, in the evening, before and after eating, and before and after any task that we do. For example, we should pray before and after studying. This kind of prayer is called "personal prayer."

On Sundays and feast days, and even on other days when we have the free time, we go to God's house to pray, to the church, where other Christians like us gather. There we pray all together, as a group. That kind of prayer is called "corporate prayer."

Chapter Twenty-One

The Fasts

In order to have more time and strength for prayer, Christians have established certain times for fasting. A fast day is a day when we take a break from our usual habits. Even the engine of a car can get worn out if it runs too much. The same is true of our soul. Day after day, our soul is busy helping us make our way through this world. During a fast, our soul can rest a little from its cares, from studying, work, and even from entertainment. Yes, we can even get tired of entertainment, tired to death. And that "death" is eternal if it kills our soul. What do we, as Christians, do during a fast? The most important thing is that we train ourselves. In other words, it is not your parents that are training you, but you yourself. You should try not to get annoyed, not to offend or hurt anyone, but rather to be helpful to everyone. Read the Gospel. And when you try this, you will discover that training yourself is hard.

To make it easier, even though it might sound strange at first, we need to begin by eating less. We stop eating meat, eggs, and milk (ie non-fasting foods) and we eat only "fasting" food, foods that come from plants – bread, fruits, vegetables, etc. When we eat a lot of food with animal fat, instead of making us want to pray, it makes us want to sleep, or else gives us too much energy so that we want to run and jump.

Also, when it is a fast day, you can try to spend less time on the computer or watching TV. When we constantly play games and watch movies, our thoughts jump all over the place. When we avoid entertainment, we can gather our thoughts and evaluate our life and our behavior. Fasting is like a compass in the life of a Christian. From time to time, fasting allows us to check where we are going, to see where we are in our journey into the Kingdom of Heaven.

The longest fast is the one that comes before Pascha. This fast is called "Great Lent." There is also the Nativity Fast which comes before Christmas, the Apostles Fast which comes before the feast of the Apostles Peter and Paul, and the

The Dormition of the Theotokos (August 15th) is when we celebrate her earthly death and passage to eternal life. After the Theotokos died, her Son came and took her body into Heaven.

Dormition Fast, when we prepare ourselves to celebrate the Dormition of the Mother of God.

Chapter Twenty-Two

The Holy Icons

Icons are depictions of the Lord God Himself, the Theotokos, the angels, or of holy people.

God is Spirit (John 4:24) and is invisible. However, He has appeared to holy people in visible form, so we can depict Him in icons in the forms in which He has revealed Himself. Icons of the Trinity show three Angels, sitting around a table, because the Lord once appeared to Abraham in the form of three Angels. Often, the three Angels are drawn with wings to make it clear that they are spirits, not just regular humans.

If you want to read the whole story of when the Lord appeared to Abraham in the form of three angels, it is found in the 18th chapter of Genesis.

Each of the Persons of the Holy Trinity are depicted as follows.

God the Father is depicted as an old man, the Ancient of Days, since He appeared in that form to some of the prophets.

God the Son is depicted in the form that He took on Himself when He came down on Earth and became Man for our salvation. He is shown as an Infant in the arms of His Mother. He is also shown

teaching the people and performing miracles, on the mountain at His Transfiguration, suffering on the Cross, lying in the Tomb, rising from the dead, and ascending into Heaven. Once, Jesus Christ even gave us an icon of Himself. When He had washed His face, He wiped His most-pure face with a towel and in a miraculous way, an image of His face was left on the towel for the sick King Abgar. When the king prayed before this icon of the Savior "not made by hands," he was healed of his disease.

God the Holy Spirit is depicted as a dove, because that was how He appeared when the Savior was being baptized by John the Baptist in the river Jordan. He is also depicted as tongues of fire, because that was how He came down in a visible form on the holy Apostles on the day of Pentecost, fifty days after Christ's Resurrection.

When we pray before an icon, we should remember that the icon itself is not God or a saint but only a depiction, and so we do not pray to the icon but to the person depicted on the icon.

An icon is a lot like a holy book. When we read the Bible with reverence and love, with trembling and piety, we read God's words, and we may imagine images of the stories in the Bible. When we look at a holy icon with piety, in the same way we behold the faces of Christ and the saints. Both God's Word and the holy icons raise our mind to God and His saints and ignite our heart with love for our Creator and Savior.

Chapter Twenty-Three

Who Else is Depicted in the Holy Icons, Besides God

Besides God, icons depict the Mother of God (the Theotokos), the holy Angels, and holy people (the saints). But we should not pray to them like we pray to God, but like those who are close to God, who have been pleasing to Him by their holy lives. They all pray for us before God. We should ask them for help and intercession, because God hears our sinful prayers more quickly for their sake (James 5:16). An example might help us understand. Imagine that we want to ask something from someone who is very kind but also very powerful, like a principal or someone in authority. In cases like that, we often bring someone with us that the person in authority knows well, like our mom or dad or a friend, who can vouch for us so that the person we are asking will grant our request more quickly, not just for our sake, but for the sake of those who lovingly ask with us.

First of all, we turn to the Mother of God to ask for her prayers, because she is closer than anyone else to God, and also close to us at the same time. For the sake of her maternal love and prayer,

God forgives and helps us often. She is a great and merciful intercessor for all of us!

The first icons of the Theotokos were made while she was still living on earth. One of the disciples of Jesus Christ, the Apostle Luke, was the one who made them. Some of these images have been preserved even to the present. There is a tradition that the Theotokos, when she saw her icon for the first time, said, "The grace of my Son will be with this image."

An "intercessor" means someone who asks for help on behalf of someone else or who prays for them.

Chapter Twenty-Four

The Ranks of Saints

Icons also depict holy people, the saints, "the God-pleasing." We say that they are pleasing to God, because while they lived on the Earth, they pleased God with their righteous life. And now that they abide in Heaven with God, they pray to God for us, helping us who still live on Earth. There are different ranks of saints with different titles. You may have heard some of these titles: prophet, apostle, martyr, holy hierarch, venerable, unmercenary, blessed, righteous. Let's learn what these mean.

Prophets

The prophets are those who were inspired by the Holy Spirit and predicted what was to come. They lived before the Savior came to Earth and foretold His coming.

There are relatively few prophets; most of them have books of the Bible named after them.

Apostles

The Apostles are the Lord Jesus Christ's closest disciples, whom He sent to preach even during His earthly life. After the Holy Spirit came upon them at Pentecost, they preached the Christian faith to all nations. There were twelve primary Apostles and seventy others. Two of the Apostles, Peter and Paul, are called the "Princes of the Apostles," because they labored even harder than the others in preaching the faith of Christ. Four Apostles (Matthew, Mark, Luke, and John the Theologian) wrote the Gospels and are called "**the Evangelists**."

Saints, who like the Apostles spread the Christian faith in different places to many people, are called "**Equal-to-the-Apostles**." For example, Mary Magdalene, the right-believing monarchs Constantine and Helen, Cyril and Methodius who taught and enlightened the Slavs, Grand Prince Vladimir, St. Nina the Enlightener of Georgia, and others.

Martyrs

Martyrs are those Christians who suffered harsh torment and even death for their faith in Jesus Christ. If a saint suffered torment for Christ but survived and died peacefully, we call them **confessors**.

The first saints who suffered for Christ were the Archdeacon Stephen and St. Thekla, and so they are called "**the First-martyrs**" or "**the Protomartyrs**."

Saints who died for the holy faith after especially great torment, greater than most other martyrs, are called "**Great-martyrs**." Some

> There are many, many martyrs, so many that no one except God knows the exact number. Even just counting the ones we humans know about, they are probably the largest group of saints.

examples of Great-martyrs are St. George, St. Barbara, St. Catherine, and others.

Holy Hierarchs

These saints are bishops who pleased God with their righteous lives. Some famous ones are St. Nicholas the Wonderworker, St. Alexius of Moscow, St. John Chrysostom (who wrote our most commonly used liturgy), and St. Raphael of Brooklyn.

Clergy who are martyred for Christ are called "**hieromartyrs**."

> The "hiero" part is from a Greek word meaning "priest", and means that they were ordained.

Venerable

Saints given the title of "venerable" are monastics. They left behind society and their life in the world and decided not to marry, pleasing God by living their whole lives in prayer and fasting, and living in deserts and monasteries. Some examples of this kind of saint are St. Sergius of Radonezh, St. Seraphim of Sarov, St. Mary of Egypt, Saint Herman of Alaska, and others.

Monks and nuns who suffered and died for Christ are called "venerable martyrs."

Unmercenaries

The holy unmercenaries are those saints who served their neighbors by treating their diseases without compensation. "Unmercenary" comes from a Latin word meaning "not seeking money" or "not paid." In other words, they cured people of their illnesses without accepting any kind of payment. They healed both physical and spiritual diseases. Some common examples of unmercenaries are Sts. Cosmas and Damian, the holy Great-martyr and Healer Panteleimon, and others.

Righteous

These are saints who pleased God while living in the world with families, such as Sts. Joachim and Anna, St. John of Kronstadt, and others.

The first righteous saints, the patriarchs of the human race, are called the forefathers. Adam, Noah, and Abraham are examples of this rank of saints. "Forefathers" sometimes also means any righteous person who was an ancestor of Christ.

Chapter Twenty-Five

Conclusion

Although this short book has come to an end, there is more to learn, because everything that we need to know about God cannot fit in one book. If we really want to understand why we came into this world, why things happen to us, and what is waiting for us in the future, we have to live our life with God. As you write the book of your own life, may your hand be guided by the firm and loving hand of God!

CPSIA information can be obtained
at www.ICGtesting.com
Printed in the USA
BVHW021727220919
558953BV00009B/9/P